Of Knights and Fair Maidens

A Radical New Approach
to a Very Old Way
of Developing Relationships

JEFF & DANIELLE MYERS

ABOUT THE AUTHORS

The life mission of **Jeff and Danielle Myers** is
to train future leaders to understand the times in
which they live, equipping them with the skills
they need to make a difference in the world.
Their speaking and writing ministry focuses on
apologetics, principles of godly leadership,
character development and relationships. Jeff's
spiritual gift is teaching and encouragement.
Danielle's spiritual gift is serving.

MYERS
INSTITUTE
FOR COMMUNICATION
& LEADERSHIP
**P. O. Box 7
Dayton, TN 37321
www.myersinstitute.com**

**Library of Congress Catalog Card Number: 95-95345
ISBN 0-9650538-0-6**

Contents

Rethinking Relationships

Important Steps to Great Relationships

How to "Do" Courtship

Appendices

Chapter One
So You Want to Go Back to Medieval Times?

"Could it really be him?" wondered the fair maiden, her heart pounding. She flung open the windows and watched the lone rider, far across the plain, galloping toward her father's castle. She had waited a long time, her eyes scanning the distant horizon, the faint glimmer of hope growing brighter with each passing day.

And here he was! As the horseman spurred his fine white Arab charger closer, the sun glinted off his shining armor. Self-assured, obviously victorious, the knight was at last coming to claim his bride.

The white charger's nostrils flared as his master urged him on in eager advance. It seemed like an eternity, but at last the confident rider reigned in his mount beneath her window. The fair maiden nearly fainted as she anticipated hearing his golden voice oozing with romantic vigor. The fair maiden would soon be a beautiful princess!

As the knight slowly raised his face shield, his fine features were illumined by the setting sun. "Like, hey babe," he said, sounding somewhat bored.

"Hey, babe? What kind of greeting is that?" she thought, startled.

"Like, I-have-just-arrived, like, ya' know, from the Twentieth Century," he said in a flat voice. "They have a way-cool way of doing things there, ya' know. It's like, different. But I like it, ya' know?"

"What do you mean 'It's, like, different?'" she queried, her faint voice quivering.

"Yeah, I mean, why don't we just skip all this 'knights a-courting' biz'. It's just too, like, old-fashioned, ya' know?"

"What do you have in mind?" asked the poor girl, utterly beside herself.

"Well, okay, like. . .okay. Like, ya' know, yer dad doesn't have to know or anything, but I was thinkin' we'd just grab a pizza and a movie, and see how things go from there. Who knows? Like, eventually we might just get the right vibes, ya' know, and move in together, and maybe if it works out, we could even, like, ya' know. . ."

"Like, *what?*" she asked, maintaining her calm.

"Well, you know, like, well, get m-. M- m-. M- mar-. . ."

"Get *what?*" she asked, irritated.

"M- m- mar. Mar- mar- marri-. . ."

He didn't even have to finish. The windows closed and the fair maiden disappeared inside. She looked in the mirror and sighed. "Another budding romance bites the dust!" she exclaimed to no one in particular.

On Second Thought. . .

Whatever happened to the good old days of knights and fair maidens? Where did we lose the thrill of true romance, the excitement of planning for marriage, the anticipation of a family's wholehearted approval, and the determination to stay pure until the wedding night?

"Get real," you say. "This is the *Modern Age.* Are you trying to take us back to medieval times?"

On second thought, that's not a bad idea. We *like* seeing guys who are man enough to work hard to win the hearts of their beloved. We *appreciate* the tenderness of the moment when two people realize that God has put them together. We *applaud* planning for a lifetime of wholehearted commitment to each other.

But then again, maybe we're just old fashioned.

Or are we? Every place we go we meet people from high school age into their thirties who say, "There's got to be something more to relationships than what we see on TV and in the movies." They are well-adjusted, successful, attractive people. Clearly, something about popular culture is missing the mark with these individuals, and we meet more of them all the time, looking for something *more* out of relationships than what their culture has taught them to expect.

We think there *is* something more. As of the writing of this book, we are still newlyweds, having been married for less than two years. It's been fantastic! We have avoided so many pitfalls that usually trap young married couples. We aren't experts on marriage, but we think we made some right decisions during the time before our marriage.

Our goal before we were married is the same as our goal now: to figure out how Christians can develop relationships with members of the opposite sex in a way that glorifies God and reflects the character of Jesus Christ.

"I Love You So Much I Want to Spend the Rest of My Week With You"

Unfortunately, our society seems to diminish rather than reinforce the importance of marriage and commitment. Recently we saw a newspaper article about a famous male movie star who had been coaxed away from his wife of many years to take up residence with a famous female movie star. Then, after a short while, he dumped the famous female movie star too. Shocked and hurt, she apparently believed that he was incapable of cheating on her.

In the article, the famous female movie star said something that really reflects Hollywood's current attitude toward relationships. "It was devastating," she moaned. "It's a painful thing to be rejected by someone you think you want to spend *a great deal of your time with*." (Italics ours)

Amazing. Have we gotten to the point where relationships mean so little that we cannot bring ourselves to say, "I made a commitment to this person and it hurts" or "I feel bad because I thought this was the person with whom I would spend the rest of my life"? Instead we say, "This was a person I wanted to spend a great deal of time with."

No wonder recent statistics show that the divorce rate is up more than 40% since 1970, and more than 250% since 1940. It has gotten so bad that some marriage counselors, apparently believing divorce is inevitable, developed the concept of the "starter marriage," which, like a starter house, is a place to begin but not where you hope to end up. Evidently some counselors encourage people to choose mates who can help them become financially and emotionally stable and learn about marriage so they can later "move up" to someone who is younger, more attractive, or more wealthy.

Looking Back. Way Back.

Our answer to the trend is to go in the opposite direction.

Of Knights and Fair Maidens will show you how to develop relationships in an old-fashioned, yet radically new way. We will share the story of how *our* relationship developed through what we call a *courtship*. You'll hear the story of our unique relationship through the inquiries of a "mystery interviewer" whose questions are pertinent, realistic and sometimes difficult. Through this conversation, and through the "how to" chapters that follow, you will have a chance to learn how you can build three exciting, unique qualities into the guy/girl relationships part of your life.

We have not written this book in hopes of creating a bestseller or even getting it onto the shelves of Christian bookstores. We have written it because it sparks a discussion about how Christian guys and girls can get a lot better head start on marriage than the rest of our society.

Through our discussion, you will learn some ideas that can help form the foundation of a solid relationship. You will discover how to develop true friendships, deepen your love for others, and heighten your personal impact on the world around you. You'll discover how to be a *leader* rather than a follower in the area of relationships, and you'll be challenged to think about guy/girl relationships in a whole new way.

What have we to lose by trying something new? Or something old, for that matter! Why not try something so old in fact, that it *seems* new?

So, brave knights and fair maidens, let's begin our journey!

Chapter Two
Rethinking a Very Old, But Very Cool Idea

**NOTE: To make this easier to read we will put the
questions and comments of the "mystery interviewer" in
bold, and use "J" for Jeff and "D" for Danielle to designate
who answered.**

So, what is courtship anyway?

D: Courtship, to us, is a guy/girl relationship that leads to
marriage. It focuses on three primary things:
accountability to parents and other trusted adults, building
each other's character rather than focusing on physical
attraction, and waiting to develop serious relationships until
you are really ready to get married.

I don't get it.

J: Don't worry! There is much confusion about courtship.

The important thing is that courtship recognizes that the purpose of guy/girl relationships is to prepare for marriage, so you treat it seriously right from the start. You don't look for excuses to go off by yourselves, and you bring other people, such as moms and dads, into the decisions you make. The guy starts preparing to become a spiritual leader, and works to "win the heart" of the girl.

Isn't that somewhat old-fashioned?

J: That is what I thought when I first heard about it. But I've now realized that just because something is old fashioned doesn't mean it is bad!

That is true, I guess. But will people do it?

D: The truth is, we have met many Christian young people who are committed to having their relationships reflect the character of Christ, and are *very* interested in courtship. We talk about it to high school and college students who attend public, Christian and home schools. There's a lot of interest!

Tell about how you heard of courtship.

D: I dated throughout high school and my early college years. I had heard of courtship , but I thought, "Oh, it's just another word for dating." After a few years of college, though, I was just fed up with the whole dating scene. I had gotten myself into a lot of bad dating relationships, and I was thinking, "This can't be all there is -- there must be a better way." I started to ask, "What would *God* want me to do?" I was trying to make a lot of life changes, and trying to turn *all of my life* over to God instead of just Sundays.

At that time, I started looking at what different people had to say about finding the person that you would spend the rest of your life with. I came across an article in *New Attitude* magazine entitled "Dating Problems, Courtship Solutions," and thought, "That's really interesting." Then one of my professors who home schools his children gave me a copy of John Holtzman's book, *Dating with Integrity*. It doesn't deal specifically with courtship, but it does talk about turning your relationships over to God. It also gives solid principles that you can live by.

J: I guess the first time I heard about the idea of courtship was at a home school conference about four years ago. Danielle and I had not developed a relationship. In fact, we hardly knew each other at that point, and I was dating someone else. A home school mom asked me, "Is there someone special in your life?" I replied that yes, there was. She asked, "Are you *dating* or *courting?*"

My first thought was, "Courting? You mean like old-fashioned medieval 'knight in shining armor' kind of courting? These home schoolers! What will they come up with next?" I envisioned home schoolers blowing the dust off old books and digging through them, trying to find ways that things *used* to be done -- and the older the better!

But I'm glad I gave it some more thought. I had gotten to the point in my life where I had to turn my dating life over to God. I said, "Lord, I never thought I would have to pray this, but if you want me to stay single for the rest of my life, I will." I tried to make the different parts of my life reflect that. I didn't hang around in singles groups (I have heard as many disaster stories coming out of singles groups as I have heard success stories). I started going to Sunday school classes and church groups based on the *teaching* rather than who was in the class. The Lord really began to bless that.

How did the two of you meet?

D: We met in the summer of 1993. Jeff worked full time for Summit Ministries, a leadership training camp for teenagers. I joined the Summit staff as a counselor for the summer.

J: The first time we really talked was around the dinner table with the staff at Summit Ministries. The staff really uses meal times to get to know each other. I guess it was the conversations around the dinner table that really started our relationship, which is probably not typical! Typically, a guy just look at a girl and think, "I would like to get to know that girl," based on the way she looks.

Wait. Back up. Doesn't courtship sort of assume that you marry "the girl next door" that you've known all your life?

D: We aren't experts, but I have heard of people who think that courtship can only happen in the "small town" when the families have known each other for a long time, and the young guy starts "calling" on the girl's family, sitting in the parlor with them, as a way of getting to spend time with the girl.

J: There are several problems with this scenario. First, small towns aren't what they used to be. If *we* had daughters, I'm not sure I would let some of the Christian guys in the small town where I grew up come anywhere near them! There was nothing distinctive about their lives at all. That was fifteen years ago. It's much worse now.

Another problem is that families move around a lot more. We live in Colorado Springs, which has five military bases, and most of the military personnel move every three years. It's very difficult for people to develop long term relationships in their town. In addition, most teens spend a few years in college, which takes them away from home. The fellowship and relationships they develop at college are outside the context of the family.

So, how do you resolve that problem?

J: We've tried to develop a courtship model that teens and single people in their twenties and older can use in a variety of circumstances. It focuses more on the *principles* rather than the *circumstances* in which people find themselves.

And those principles are . . .

D: Accountability, character, and preparation. We'll spend three chapters discussing them.

Chapter Three
How We Met and Committed to Marriage Before We Fell in Love

How did you progress from dinner table conversation to courtship?

D: That's a long, long story!

Give us the short version.

J: The *Dating with Integrity* book Danielle mentioned earlier suggests that Christian singles develop friendships with both guys and girls that are not exclusive, and view all unmarried Christian guys and girls as brothers and sisters in Christ. So I pursued that model, committing to do nothing with a girl that I wouldn't do with my sister. I would often ask guys and girls, whoever was available, to go with me to do things such as wash my car, go to the store, run errands, mountain bike, or whatever.

One particular evening, my two brothers were both at Summit Ministries, and I asked them if they could mountain bike with me after dinner. Neither of them could. I turned around, and Danielle was still there at the table. I asked her if she would like to mountain bike with me, and she said yes.

Uh, oh.

J: Exactly! If I had known that Danielle had never been mountain biking before, I would have chosen a different trail.

D: There *wasn't* a trail. It was erosion on the side of a mountain!

J: Well, we got to the top of the mountain on a road, and I wanted to take this "trail" back down. I said, "This trail is pretty rough," which apparently is not as descriptive as it should be. Anyway, I asked, "Do you still want to do it?" Danielle said yes (she says yes to most challenges since she's so adventurous). Next thing I knew, I was at the bottom of the trail, because it was pretty much straight down.

D: Every time I fell, and there were many times, I slid down the mountain a little bit more, and eventually got back on my bike. By the time I made it to the bottom, I had blood running down my knees and my hands -- I was a wreck.

J: I asked, "Danielle, are you okay?" She said, "Yes, I'm fine," and rode right by!

D: I didn't even stop. But it did give new meaning to falling head-over-heels for someone!

J: It rained on us the rest of the way home that night.

D: That's right!

J: But there was one good thing that came out of that experience. When you're mountain biking and its pouring down rain and you're hurt, you get to know the real person. It really tears off the masks that you tend to put on to impress people.

This is turning into the long version.

J: Okay, okay. The turning point in our relationship was when, about a week later, I asked Danielle if she would like to mountain bike with me again, and she said "yes." So I knew that this was the kind of adventurous person I was looking for!

But how did you progress to courtship?

D: We did other things together that summer, mostly in groups, as we'll talk about when we get to the "character" issue. But in courtship, there comes a point when you recognize that this is the person that God has chosen for you. You make that decision based on the godly character of the other person, the goals that they have, and the "green lights" that you get from your parents and other older adults that you trust.

You're kidding. What about the emotions of "being in love"?

J: We've thought a lot about that. Here is a question we've struggled with: "Why are emotions more reliable than your assessment of a person's character?"

D: We have concluded that emotions are actually less reliable. Emotions come and go; they change all the time. If you rely on emotions to tell you whether you are "in love," you are probably in for a really bumpy marriage.

So you didn't have feelings of being in love at that time?

D: Actually, no.

J: Danielle's right. True attraction comes out of falling in love with someone's character, not falling in love with how handsome or beautiful they are. It takes longer, but it is a whole lot more reliable. When Danielle smiles at me, I get goose bumps. She has a really pretty smile, but I fell in love with her smile because I knew that it came from deep inside -- she's a woman of character.

I want to hear about how you knew each other's character so well. But first, let's get back to the story. How did you get to the point of talking about marriage?

J: Our big "conversation" came toward the end of the summer. It started out as another one of my infamous wilderness guide disasters. I took Danielle on a hike so we could visit. Unfortunately, I severely underestimated how long it would take to hike the trail I had chosen, so I found myself leading Danielle through scrub brush and up rock formations trying to find a short cut. By the time we found our way it was about 9:30 p.m., and dark. As we came back down the mountain, I finally got up the courage to ask the "big question." Not the *really* big question, engagement, but the big one, courtship.

How did you ask it?

J: I said, "Danielle, when I was your age I would have been afraid to hear what I am about to say. But you are the kind of person that I would like to have for a wife. I understand if that scares you."

D: It didn't scare me at all because I had seen character qualities in Jeff that I wanted in a husband.

J: So I said, "What I would like to do is ask your father permission to court you until marriage."

What did that mean to you?

J: At that point, in my mind, I was committing to marriage. It didn't mean engagement, of course, but it *was* a commitment to marriage. I knew I could make that commitment based on what I knew of Danielle's character.

Could you get out of it?

D: We didn't see courtship as binding in the sense that we couldn't get out of it, but we did see it as a serious commitment to pursue the kind of relationship that would lead to marriage.

How did you approach Danielle's father?

J: A couple of weeks later, I called Danielle's father and asked to spend a day with him. I drove from Colorado Springs to

Wichita, Kansas, to see him. We worked together for a few hours in his inner city ministry. Eventually, we came to the part of the day where I knew it was time for "the talk." I asked if he would like to go get a soft drink. My heart was nearly pounding right out of my chest.

How did he respond?

J: Danielle's dad is a really nice guy.

D: He's also very direct!

J: And that helped in this situation! He said, "It's obvious that we're not just here to look at each other." I thought, "I'm 27 years old -- this should not be a part of relationships anymore!" But I understood that we had to be accountable to our parents. So I said, "I am very interested in your daughter. She's a beautiful girl in her appearance, but I mostly appreciate who she is in her character -- who she is as a person. I would like to ask your permission to court your daughter until marriage."

What did he say?

J: He asked, "What do you mean by *court?*" I explained it as best I could. When I finished, he said, "I don't think I understand what that is, but if that is what you guys want to do, that's fine with me." I breathed a sigh of relief.

D: Just a minute too soon.

J: Then he threw me. He asked, "Why haven't you kissed my daughter?" I nearly swallowed my tongue.

D: My papa and I talk about everything!

J: I also realized how odd the idea of courtship is. It had not occurred to me to kiss Danielle in the course of our friendship. I mean, it had occurred to me as a guy, but it had not occurred to me as part of our relationship, because we were working on character and staying away from the physical stuff. So I explained to him that before I had come to Christ, I had lived a certain way in my life that made it very important for me to maintain absolute physical purity in every aspect of our relationship. I think he honored and appreciated that. That was really the beginning of a friendship for us. Even if Danielle is not there, her father and I can spend time together.

D: That was really the beginning of our relationship. In fact, that was how we started developing the first of the three principles we want to discuss in this book, accountability.

J: The next chapter is called "Breaking the 'Lone Ranger' Habit" because we have come to realize that when a couple separates themselves from contact with everyone else to develop a relationship, they have a harder time being accountable and miss out on so much of what makes a courtship great.

Chapter Four
Breaking the "Lone Ranger" Habit

Explain the basis for the principle of accountability.

D: We disagree with the typical dating game where the couple gets together, shows up at home, and announces, "Here we are, like it or not" to the parents. We wanted our relationship to be different. So instead, we went to our parents and asked permission, requesting their guidance at every step. Because our parents are older and wiser, we knew that they could guide us and help us avoid making wrong decisions along the way.

J: We were also accountable to *each other's* parents. When I met with Danielle's father the first time, I told him, "I would like to be accountable to you in this relationship, and I want to put myself under your authority as it regards your daughter. And at any point during our relationship, you can call me and ask any question, any question about *anything,* and I will answer you honestly."

Why is the relationship with family so important?

J: When you get married, you don't just marry another person.
You marry a whole family. If the family's not happy, there
is automatically tension in the relationship. I saw a study
recently that indicated that tension with in-laws is a major
cause of instability in the marriage.

D: So the lesson is if you're not getting along with the family,
step back from the whole thing and work on that
relationship first. The Bible tells us to honor our parents.
Making sure they are a part of your important life decisions
is a very significant way of honoring them.

**How do you exercise accountability when your parents are
not around?**

D: That's a great question, because I was at school in another
state, not living at home, and Jeff was in Colorado several
hours drive from *his* parents. I had a lady in my church
who met with me for discipleship almost every week. She
asked me questions to help me stay on the right track. I, of
course, had a lot of questions for her.

J: Ditto. I had a older man in Colorado Springs that I had an
accountability relationship with as well. He gave me lots of
wise counsel.

D: We also spent time with other adult couples. We received
almost all of our marriage counseling from older couples
who have been married for a long time, and even some who
have been married for a short time and knew some of the

immediate challenges we would face.

J: For example, with Danielle's mentor's family, we went over to their house and fixed dinner for them. That's the kind of thing we did instead of "dates." It's a lot more fun than seeing a movie or whatever.

D: Sometimes we went out on "double dates" with our parents. It sounds strange, but because of the accountability principle, we could spend time having fun with our parents. They provided a measure of understanding God's will in our relationship.

J: We were apart for much of that year. We were only able to get together about six times, so the temptation was mighty big to just go off by ourselves and focus on each other. Having planned activities with these older couples and our families helped us keep our focus in the right place.

Won't parents take advantage of that opportunity to put your relationship in chains?

D: It didn't work that way for us at all. Most parents set big restrictions when they feel that you are doing something wrong. When you sit down with them and say, "I want you to be involved in my life in the area of relationships, this is how I want you to guide me, and these are the ways that I want you to help me make decisions" and if they can see that you are serious, it builds trust. Trust leads to an appropriate amount of freedom.

J: Keep in mind, too, that your parents are not your enemy. Instead of it being *you* against *them*, they help you along in the right direction.

D: Both our parents gave us the full green light, which helped confirm that our relationship was the Lord's will. Because we had focused on character, and because we had a right relationship with our parents, we didn't have a lot of the "pre-wedding jitters" which plague so many couples. Neither of us were wondering at the last minute, "Is this the right thing?" It was great!

How did your parents convey their support?

J: One day as I was talking with my dad on the telephone, he said, "I think your mother likes Danielle." I asked why he thought that. He said, "Because this morning after breakfast, she asked 'Is there anything in the Bible about a mother being able to *command* her son to marry a certain person?'" I thought, "All right! Danielle is the first girl to get my mother's full endorsement!"

D: My parents showed their support by letting Jeff be in our professionally produced family photographs a full three months before we were even engaged! Of course, they took some extras without him just in case . . . .

J: "Courtship" was such a new idea, no one was quite sure how to respond!

D: We have a lot of practical ideas that we'll share in the "How to Involve Others in Your Relationship" chapter. But let's talk about focusing on character next.

Chapter Five
No Masks

The issue of "character" has already come up. But let's dig into it some more.

D: A lot of dating is "putting your best foot forward," which means that you show the other person only the very best side of you. It's pretty easy, generally, because you can put your best foot forward for two, three or even four hours if it is a long date. The other person may not even get to know the "real you" until they have made some commitments that are difficult to break.

J: My goal during our courtship was to win Danielle's heart. So I took the initiative to design activities that, among other things, would demonstrate that I was a responsible person who could be trusted and respected. We already mentioned that when we were near family, we were rarely by ourselves. My parents included Danielle in our family activities. She even came camping with us once. When our parents and brothers and sisters weren't around, most the activities we did were group oriented: ball games, picnics, working together, eating dinner with the Summit Ministries staff, and hiking together in groups. We still took hikes together and things like that, just the two of us, but we were careful not to be together without a planned activity or in a setting that would invite temptation.

D: Those kinds of activities are hard to do while "wearing masks," so to speak. You get to know what the other person is really like when you are together with a group and with their family.

J: I also worked hard to develop ministry opportunities for us. I received Danielle's father's permission to lead her in a Bible study of the five character qualities mentioned in First Timothy 4:12 -- speech, conduct, faith, love and purity. We devised activities to practice each of those.

Give us an example of what kind of activities you did together.

J: Well, for instance, I led Danielle in an evangelism project. We talked to several people, including a homeless man who asked us for money. We took him to a restaurant to get him something to eat, and visited with him and witnessed to him. That was far more rewarding than any typical date!

D: The point isn't so much what activities you engage in, but where your focus is. We used verses like II Timothy 2:22 which says to *flee* evil desires of youth and *pursue* righteousness, faith and love.

J: We talked a lot about how it is important in a Christian relationship for the guy to be the spiritual leader. When a couple gets married, the guy *represents* Christ to the girl. Before marriage, he has been given a limited right to do that by her father. When I began working on spiritual leadership in the relationship, and refrained from getting us involved in a more physical way, a spiritual bond developed. The result was that instead of having a "crush" on me, Danielle developed *respect* for me. This eased our transition into marriage in ways we probably don't even fully understand yet.

How do you avoid physical involvement in a relationship?

J: To talk about "avoiding" physical involvement makes it sound as if you are on the defense against it. The best way is to take the *offense,* which means planning activities that are centered around others and which limit the opportunities for physical involvement. Also, *talk with each other* about the standards you are setting. Danielle and I did not kiss until the night we were engaged -- that was the standard that we had set for ourselves. We held each other accountable to it, and recognized situations when we *felt* like we wanted to become physically involved, learning to *change* the situation. For example, we never cuddled up on the couch to watch a movie together. I know that sounds silly, but a lot of couples put themselves right into that situation, and end up making a screen play of their own which they later regret.

D: We wouldn't say that there are definite rules you have to follow such as, "You cannot kiss until you are married," or "You can't go off to an event just the two of you." But it is clear from Scripture that God has set guidelines that we are to follow. So if you feel like cuddling up on the couch to watch a movie, be honest: you *know* that one thing will lead to another. Ask yourself "Why am I doing this? Is this bringing glory to God? Is this giving a good witness for our relationship and for the person that I'm going to marry? *Is this how I want to conduct myself in God's presence?*"

Now, the hard part. How do you recognize godly character in someone?

D: One way of learning about the other person's character is to watch them in action. For example, the way a guy treats his mother is the way he will treat his wife, and the way a girl treats her father is the way she will treat her husband. Also, watch the person in groups. Listen to them pray or lead a Bible study, or interact with those around them.

J: It sounds strange to say it, but if you can observe how the person responds to difficult situations, you will learn more about them than you ever imagined. For example, to work on the Summit Ministries summer camp staff is one of the most difficult jobs I'm aware of. It's an extremely stressful job. During her time there, Danielle passed with flying colors. She became stronger and deeper and more patient and compassionate as the summer went on.

How did the fact that much of your relationship was long distance affect your focus on character development?

J: We have stacks of letters! Hundreds of pages! We wrote about two letters and two E-mail messages each week for nine months. I was never a letter writer before meeting Danielle. For me, writing helped me define some of my thoughts about our relationship. It helped me grow in commitment to Danielle, just through the things I was writing. And of course I would read her letters over and over again. Our letters were not just about "current events."

We intentionally included glimpses of our thought life, questioning and discussing topics that are important outside of the daily grind. By the way, I suggest to others that if their relationship is not long distance, that they write letters to each other anyway, and record their thoughts about the relationship in a journal. It will help define the relationship and give an objective way to think about it.

D: The long distance nature of our relationship was a blessing in that it forced us to focus on real issues instead of just gazing at each other and doing the things that people do when they see each other every day -- which is basically waste time. We made up lists of questions to ask each other, and did a Bible study together long distance. So when we talked on the telephone we really had something to say; it wasn't dreamy, mushy talk the whole time.

J: We've given lots more ideas for character-building in the upcoming chapter entitled "Beyond Pizza and a Movie." But it is now time for us to address the most difficult issue of all, avoiding serious relationships until you are prepared for marriage.

Chapter Six
Waiting in the Wings

Let me get this straight. Are you suggesting that people wait until they are *prepared* for marriage before they actually begin seriously pursuing a relationship?

J: Well, yes. In his *New Attitude* article entitled "Dating Problems, Courtship Solutions," Joshua Harris uses the analogy of shopping. He compares dating before you are ready to get married to window shopping with no money. You raise all kinds of desires that you cannot fulfill, and you invest all your emotional and spiritual energy into something that cannot pay off without dire consequences.

D: You shop when you are ready to buy!

What does that mean?

J: Well, in my case, I made the commitment to the Lord that I would not begin pursuing marriage until I was established in my career. That took a long time because I was a full time student working on a masters degree and then a doctorate. I was 26 before I had the salary to support a wife and one or two children. The payoff for Danielle and me has been great. We have had no arguments about money -- the whole issue has been erased for us. It's not that we have a lot of money, but that we have enough to be secure.

D: The number one reason marriages get into trouble is over finances.

J: My parents taught me that. They were married during their senior year of college -- and I was conceived on their honeymoon. When they graduated, my dad got a job in a faraway state that he had never even visited. He borrowed money to buy a car, stowed all of his earthly possessions in the back seat, and hit the road with his pregnant wife. They were still living in a motel when I was born, looking for a place to live. They said, "Whatever you do, don't repeat our first year of marriage!"

D: Song of Solomon 2:7 talks about not awakening desires before its time and Proverbs 24:27 talks about preparing your fields before you build your house. You develop a career, find a way to make money, and then build your "house," which we interpret as your marriage and family. It's common sense. But it requires patience, and people are often not willing.

If what you're saying is true, then most guys and girls will have to postpone serious relationships until much later than they are accustomed to.

J: I know that sounds unusual, but consider this: if you are between the ages of 16 and 25, you have more physical energy, more creative energy, and more opportunities for becoming an active Christian during this time of your life than you will ever have again. Don't blow it by investing all of your time, energy and money in relationships that are just for fun. Make it meaningful. Look back in history to see what others have accomplished at this time of life. George Washington was a commander in an army by age 23, something that was not uncommon in that day. He gained experience, learned to lead, and settled down later in his twenties.

D: Even if it is the right person at the wrong time, it's still the wrong person. Until you're ready to make that commitment, focus on what the Lord's will is for your life at that moment, and how to build your relationship with Him.

But how? What should young people do instead?

D: Make friends -- really good, quality friendships, especially with people of the same sex. Treat every Christian as a brother or sister in the Lord. Also, don't *try* to get into dating relationships if you aren't prepared. It causes you to have a divided mind. Instead, focus all of your energy on serving the Lord and doing what he wants you to do, and he will bring you to the place where you are ready to be with that one person.

J: One simple way to do that is to learn what you can do to make a difference in the world. Danielle and I both participated in the Summit Ministries summer leadership program. We were trained in the biblical Christian worldview and how to be active in our faith. We learned how to invest the energy we had while single into things that really count.

Can you describe how this worked in your own experience?

D: In fact, that's what we plan to do in the next chapter!

Chapter Seven
How to Fall in Love, Courtship Style

Okay, now it's time to tell us the rest of the story.

J: A lot of people probably think by now that Danielle and I
    ignored the emotions and only thought about coldly logical
    aspects of relationships. That just isn't true. But it *is* true
    that love is based on commitment, not on emotions. When
    we started our courtship, we made the *decision* to love each
    other. It's a trite saying but it's true; love is not a feeling,
    it's an act of the will.

D: We were definitely committed to each other. But we didn't
    know what came next in courtship. We had talked about the
    important issues, we knew each other's character really
    well, we had focused on ministry activities, and our parents
    were all for it. It was time to decide what was to happen
    next.

J: I knew that the next move was mine, since I was the spiritual leader in the relationship. I knew we were to be married, but I didn't know how to do engagement. I was asking myself, If you already know you're going to be married, how is engagement *different* from a typical relationship? I asked others and found very little help, because few others had tried this before.

What did you do?

J: Since we first read about courtship from Joshua Harris' *New Attitude* magazine, I called Josh, hoping he might be able to offer some sage advice. At that time, Josh was eighteen years old. I called him and said, "Our courtship's going really well, and I want you to know that I really appreciate your article because it started us down a new path -- a new way of having a relationship. The problem is, I'm not sure where to go next." As I said, I was hoping that he would offer some advice. He said, "Well, that's very interesting. As soon as you get it figured out, let me know and we will write an article on it!" I knew at that point I would be blazing my own trail. So I took a couple of days off from work, drove to Kansas, and talked and prayed about it with my father. Then I visited Danielle's father, asking his permission to marry his daughter. He gave an enthusiastic "yes!" Everyone was so excited, I thought Danielle might find out before I had a chance to surprise her. I returned to Colorado, bought an engagement ring, and began planning our engagement ceremony.

D: Jeff and I had talked several months before about whether or not he should get an engagement ring for me when the time came. Some Christian friends of ours had decided not to, donating the money instead to a worthy cause.

J: We thought it was a noble gesture, and actually thought about doing that as well. After discussing it with our families, however, we concluded that an engagement ring would be appropriate. It is a visible symbol of the commitment made, showing others that "this one is set apart." Also, it is a sign of honor, and I wanted to begin honoring my wife-to-be right from the very beginning.

D: The night Jeff asked me to marry him was unforgettable. He had planned it so that it caught me completely by surprise. He wrote a song for me, and played it on the piano and sang. Well, *sing* is not quite the right word.

J: Honey, that's not very nice!

D: No, I mean that we were both so overcome by the emotions of the moment that we were alternately laughing and crying. By the end of the song, Jeff's mouth moved, but nothing came out!

J: It was overwhelming to see this beautiful courtship move into a new stage. Danielle came and sat next to me on the piano bench. I said, "Let's make it official. Will you marry me?" She said yes!

D: That was the first time we kissed.

J: People have told us, "It's not *that* important that you don't kiss before you get engaged." But for us, it was very meaningful. If you withhold physical contact and are disciplined, it means so much more. I mean, it was really great! I had never in my life thought that a kiss would mean so much. It added an innocence to our relationship. The self-discipline mixed with the anticipation made it a really special time.

D: Others have told us that their goal is to have their first kiss during the wedding ceremony. That would be really great! Anyway, we were married about 10 months after Jeff first asked my father for permission to court me, and about four months after we got engaged. The week before our wedding was a lot of fun and our families got along really well. Even then we never looked for an excuse to get off by ourselves. We always took a brother, sister, mom or dad with us.

J: We should say that we didn't make a huge deal out of it if it didn't work out that way. I heard of one couple who had someone follow them in another car whenever they went someplace together. We didn't do that. The important thing is that we weren't looking for ways to just focus on each other.

Any final advice?

D: If you can learn anything from our experience, great! But the important thing is to be tuned in to what God says in his Word. Before you decide to get into a relationship, take time to get into the Scriptures and write down the guidelines that ought to surround the relationship.

J: If your focus is on pursuing what is good, pure and righteous, then the relationship is so beautiful when it comes together. It has been so neat to see how God has taken care of us in every part of our relationship. We have seen Him work in so many ways, financially and otherwise. We would not trade the way our relationship worked for anything. We would encourage you to make this kind of courtship more than just an idea.

D: There are so many things we could talk about, but basically most people know what they ought to do. It's just a matter of making the commitment. If you're a single person and you want to get married someday into a relationship that really works, then pursue a *godly* relationship. And remember, it is more important to *be* the right person than to *find* the right person. Trust God for that find.

J: Guys, give up the macho idea that girls want a buffed, good looking guy. If that is what they want, you can be sure that their heart is in the wrong place and you don't want to come within a country mile of them anyway. Danielle and I meet teenage girls, beautiful young women of godly character, who have as their primary qualification for a husband that he be a strong spiritual leader. That's far more important than physical attributes and talent.

Any words for parents?

J: Yes. Dads, it is never too early to start developing the kind of relationship with your kids that will cause them to *want* to pursue godly relationships. If there is a tension right now, it is your responsibility to work through it and turn your heart towards your children, so that someday they will turn their hearts towards you.

D: Pray that your children will be wise in their relationship decisions. Start praying as soon as they're born that God will prepare the proper mate for them. Also, let your children *know* that you are praying for them. It may be the one thing that keeps them secure in the stormy world around us. One mother told her children that she always prayed that God would reward them when they followed His will and punish them when they didn't. Her prayer provided incredible guidance in their lives!

In closing, say a word about your wedding day.

J: Danielle and I were married on June 11, 1994. I wish you could have been there -- our wedding was so joyous, such an incredible celebration, that even our non-Christian friends afterward said things like, "You have been a real inspiration to us." They were deeply moved by our commitment. I have a friend who is the ultimate macho man --a real tough guy -- I saw him cry for the first time in my life. It wasn't that Danielle and I are so great, it is just that what we did is so . . . *different.* It set us apart and gave us a ministry together -- right from our wedding day!

It *sounds* fantastic. I can't wait until the next part of this book -- where you will give the practical ideas about how to make a relationship like that happen.

D: That's exactly what we hope to do. We've entitled this next section, "Okay, Smart Guy!"

Chapter Eight
Okay, Smart Guy!

How did you ever come up with a chapter title like "Okay, Smart Guy!"?

J: I'm the kind of person who, when listening to a speaker with "great theories" always stands up and asks, "Okay, smart guy, how do we do it?"

D: You actually say "smart guy"?

J: Well, not actually, it's sort of a figure of speech that I keep in my head. But I figure if the speaker's idea is so good, it ought to be practical. It's reminds me of the wise, hard-working hillbilly whose poor friends were always approaching him with "can't lose" business deals to try and steal hard earned money. He stopped them every time with one question.

D: And that question is?

J: He'd look them in the eye and drawl, "If you' so smart, why ain't you rich?"

D: Maybe we should apply that story before we get too far off track.

J: Okay, here goes. We've decided to offer ideas for putting the principles we've discussed into practice. Some of these we tried in our courtship, and others we thought up later or heard about from other people. In fact, some of these ideas we *wish* we had known about in our relationship. But I guess the next best thing is to pass them on.

D: We wouldn't claim to have all revealed knowledge, so this shouldn't be considered a complete list of ideas. But it *is* a good place to start.

J: I've also stuck in something for guys on how to develop a relationship with the girls' father, since this is one of the most important things you'll ever do.

Chapter Nine

Involving Others in Your Relationship

How do you become accountable to parents?

J: After I met with my father and Danielle's father, Danielle
and I spent time together with both sets of parents. We just
took them out for coffee and talked about how we wanted to
structure our relationship in accountability to them. Ideally,
parents would initiate this. But in our case, the idea of
courtship was so new that none of us really knew what to
do. Even so, our parents were *very* receptive and told lots
of stories about their own relationships, the good and the
bad, and gave lots of great ideas and encouragement.

D: There really is no trick to this one, outside of the fact that in
today's society it is unpopular to submit to the will of your
parents. In order for courtship to work, you have to believe
that they really *do* have your best interests at heart, and then
trust God to work through them.

Jeff, how should a guy develop a relationship with his father?

J: Outline for your father what you hope to accomplish in the relationship, ask for his advice and prayer, and commit to being accountable to him. My father had permission to ask any question he wanted to ask, at any time, about my thought life, how I was proceeding in my goals for the relationship, and anything else he felt was relevant. Just knowing that he *could* call helped me stay on track.

Danielle, how should a girl develop a relationship with her father?

D: As we've said already, your relationship with your father tells you a lot about how you will treat your husband. Do you respect and honor your father? Are you willing to submit to his authority? Do you spend time with him? Think of some ideas for doing so even if it is just going along on one of his favorite activities. I always loved accompanying my father on hikes and going to auctions and soccer games with him.

Jeff, how should a guy develop a relationship with his mother?

J: We believe it is generally true that the way you treat your mother is the way you will end up treating your wife. Start by expressing gratefulness for the things your mother has done for you. Esteem her for the time, energy, blood, sweat and tears she has put into your life. Take her out for a nice lunch, help with household tasks, and spend time visiting. You'll never regret it.

Danielle, how should a girl develop a relationship with her mother?

D: What Jeff said about mothers applies to mother/daughter relationships as well. But it is also important for a girl to talk with her mother about "life lessons" she has learned, and ask her advice on situations you encounter. Help her out around the house. Spend time with her and her friends, if possible.

What if you're a long way from home, or if you want additional accountability?

J: If you are out of the home, working or attending school in another city, or just desire additional accountability, consider developing a relationship with an older person of the same sex. This is called "mentoring," and it is what the Apostle Paul did for Timothy, and what Timothy admonished the older women in his church to do for the younger women. Mentoring relationships serve many functions:

   ▸ Bible study (either he teaches or you study together and share).
   ▸ Accountability (allowing him to ask tough questions).
   ▸ Advice (listening to his wisdom about dealing with difficult situations or preparing for the future).

D: Getting a mentor is not a replacement for developing the relationships with your parents. In fact, it would be best if your parents are in on the process of choosing a mentor.

How do you get started in a mentoring relationship?

D: We think there are five basic steps:

Step One

Pray that God will bring the right person to you.

Step Two

Guys, ask your father and your pastor who they would recommend. They probably know some men who are strong in their faith, share similar interests with you, and would be willing to meet with you. Girls, ask your mother and your pastor's wife. They have great access to women in the church and probably knows a woman who would be just right.

Step Three

Outline your expectations. Where will you meet? How often would you like to meet? What will you do during that time? Will you have a Bible study together, or will it just be for the purposes of accountability?

Step Four

Make an appointment, preferably at a restaurant if you're a guy (starting in a neutral location makes it more comfortable for guys).

Step Five

Stay committed. Don't break your appointments, and don't neglect to prepare for your time together. If you don't feel like you have anything to talk about, use some of the questions in the preparation section of this book to ask for advice.

J: Bringing accountability to your relationship helps ensure that you are not going to be a "lone ranger" in developing a relationship. If your relationship is just between you and the person you are interested in it is going to be a lot harder to resolve problems when they arise, figure out what to do in difficult times, or avoid temptation as you draw closer together. You need someone who can ask you hard questions, keep you thinking, help you avoid dangerous situations, and challenge you to *become* the right person. Since this is especially important for guys, I've jotted down some ideas about how to maintain accountability with the girl's father in the next chapter.

Chapter Ten
Just For Guys: How to Get to Know Her Dad

Obviously, you two place a big emphasis on getting to know the father of the girl you want to marry. You told earlier about things *you* did in your relationship. Can you expand on those?

J: Well first, you've got to get up the nerve to go talk with him. Here are some ideas for what to talk about and how to initiate the conversation. I did many of these things, and learned about others after I had already talked with Danielle's father. Of course, it works a lot better if you live close together. If not, just do as much as you can.

> ▸ Take him out for a meal. A meal in a neutral location (such as a restaurant).
> ▸ Think of questions to ask. You don't have to write them down, but think of them in advance.

- Get to know his hobby. Ask if you can observe or go along.
- Do something out-of-doors. Go fishing, hunting, boating, cycling or hiking together.
- Have a Bible study. If he has time and is willing, get together on a regular basis to study God's Word. There are many great resources in the Christian bookstore for men's Bible studies.
- Help him around the house.
- Go to work with him for a day.
- Do a sporting activity together. Go play golf or tennis, or attend a sporting event.
- Participate in a community service project together.
- Ask him to teach you a practical skill such as auto maintenance or home repair.
- Participate in his men's Bible study if he has one.

So, what kind of questions do you ask?

J: The point of these questions is to help you get to know the father better, and discern his goals for his daughter. The *thought* behind the question is more important than the wording, so relax -- don't feel pressured to structure every situation or maximize every moment. Here are some questions that get beyond "yes" or "no" answers and create discussion.

- What are your goals for your daughter's life?
- What do you consider to be the most important thing in life?
- What hobbies do you have or what do you enjoy spending time on?
- What is a really good book that you recommend?
- How did you meet your wife?

- What kind of advice would you give to a young couple who is interested in pursuing a relationship?
- What are some of the lessons you have learned about marriage?
- What are some of the most important lessons you have learned about business?
- What are some of the most important lessons you have learned about life?
- Tell me about where you grew up.
- Tell me about a favorite childhood memory.
- Tell me about your favorite family memories.
- Tell me about an exciting place you have been.
- If you could do one thing to change the world, what would you do?
- Describe the most adventurous thing you have ever done.

Won't her father feel threatened by this?

J: If he is not familiar with the idea of courtship, he may be confused at first, and may wonder *why* you're doing this. However, the guys I've worked with in the area of courtship have discovered that the father quickly warms up to the idea and is happy to get to know a young man who has integrity. You see, most fathers want their daughter to be *happy*. So if this part of the relationship will do that, he'll work with you in it.

What if he doesn't?

J: The point is not that everything in a courtship run "by the book," but that you make a strong effort to do things in the right way. If the girl's father doesn't warm up to the idea of having a relationship with you, then do your best to maintain a friendly association and find another older man to mentor you.

So what's next?

J: That's all we can cover on accountability in the short space we have. Next, we'll look into how to stretch for more and *expect* more in the course of the relationship by focusing on building character.

Chapter Eleven

Beyond Pizza and a Movie

What is involved in learning about the character of the other person and building character together through your relationship?

D: This section could be a book in itself, there is so much you can do. Instead, we've decided to keep it simple and limit our analysis to two things. The first is how to really get to know the other person. The second is how to grow together through ministry opportunities.

Are you suggesting that the couple spend time alone together?

J: Some people who talk about courtship think that is altogether bad. We don't necessarily think so, although we *do* stress that a healthy courtship is one in which you enjoy *all* of the relationships in both of your lives. If courting is preparation for life, then whether your adventures involve brothers and sisters, friends, or parents, you can have a great time and learn a lot about how the other person handles different kinds of situations.

D: We *do* say this, however: If you find yourself *looking* for excuses to be alone with the other person, be careful. It may be that your selfish desire to "have the other person all to yourself" is taking over, and that's not healthy.

It looks like you have a ton of ideas. Where did you get them all?

D: Most of these ideas are from a list given to me by Dr. Lee Griffith, a psychology professor at Anderson University and a home school dad. They are all "non-traditional" activities that people can engage in, getting to know each other in fun, creative ways. You can also take someone else, or a couple of people along. You can even go with one or more of your parents. Some of them are a riot!

- Play games.
- Go to church functions together.
- Go to the lake for a day.
- Make a fancy dinner together.
- Volunteer at a nursing home, jail, or community clean up activity.
- Do landscaping and yard work at your church, or at the home of someone who needs help.
- Visit all of the nearby tourist sights you've never bothered to check out.
- Have a cookout.
- Tour something: a ship, bakery, dairy, or radio/TV station.

- Plant a garden.
- Visit a fine arts museum.
- Go to the library and research some crazy topic.
- Go Christmas caroling, even at odd times of the year.
- Hike, mountain bike, roller blade, cross country ski, jog, or ice skate.
- Run errands for someone.
- Visit a used bookstore.
- Have a "bigger and better" night, where you start with something small and go door to door asking them to give you something that is "bigger and better" than what you have.
- Buy some paints and paint a picture.
- Throw a theme party for friends.
- Write a story together and try to get it published.
- Lead singing on an elevator or in another public place.
- Visit a junkyard.
- Shop for something special: fancy china, a car, or a mink coat (don't buy anything!).
- Go bowling with friends.
- Attend an unusual convention of stamp collectors, coin collectors, home improvement experts, or Elvis Presley look-a-likes.
- Price caskets at a funeral home.
- Buy a junk piece of furniture and refinish it.
- Go to an auction.
- Visit a large toy store.
- Go garage "saling."
- Visit a farmer's market.

What kinds of activities can you do together to *build* character?

J: We've got a big list of these as well. Before we get to

them, let me say this: Danielle and I believe that the *guy* should begin the process, with the permission of the girl's father, of becoming the spiritual leader in the relationship. This transition is not complete until marriage, but the girl will learn to respect the guy more if he has her best interests in mind and if he can begin practicing the skills he needs to lead a family. Here are some activities that Dr. Griffith suggested mixed with things we tried or thought up:

- Babysit the children of a couple who needs some "date time" (be extremely careful not to put yourselves in an environment that allows for temptation).
- Earn some money raking leaves, shoveling snow, or washing windows.
- Fold bulletins for your church, or help out in other ways.
- Sit in on a trial and discuss it afterwards.
- Write letters to missionaries.
- Visit a cemetery and read gravestones. Talk about the lives those people might have lived.
- Become a Big Brother/Big Sister.
- Conduct "Creation" tours of a zoo or museum, using information you've gained from books about Creationism.
- Make up a survey (on anything) and give it at the mall or in a park.
- Teach a Sunday school class.
- Fix a meal for a couple with a new baby.
- Make crafts for birthday or Christmas presents.
- Read a really good book.
- Study I Timothy 4:12 together, analyzing each of the areas where the Apostle Paul told Timothy to "set an example" for the believers. Think of activities you could do together and separately to do that.

- Visit a Christian bookstore.
- Go to the public library.
- Conduct an evangelism activity.
- Take a group of children on a field trip.
- Make some bag lunches and distribute them to homeless people.
- Create a leaflet to hand out at sports events -- put the players names and positions on one side, and the testimony of Christian athletes on the other.
- Volunteer for a political party.
- Go to a conference or seminar together.
- Plan a budget together.
- Draw house plans of houses you'd like to build. Compare them.

The possibilities are endless, aren't they?

D: Actually, yes. These lists are just a start. Each person reading this book probably has creative ideas of his own.

J: In fact, we'd like to hear about them. It would be fun to make a great big list that we could share with everyone.

D: Well, now it is time to go on to the last section, on how to prepare for marriage. We've divided this section into two chapters. The *first* one is on stuff to *think* about in preparing for marriage. The *second* is on things to *talk* about.

Chapter Twelve

Getting Ready, Part One:
Stuff to Think About

It has been said that most young people don't prepare well enough for marriage because when they're in love, they're blind to many of the practical issues they will face. Is that true?

D: If you "fall in love" with someone, it changes the way you think.

J: I think most people *stop* thinking! I've heard a lot of starry-eyed people, not just teenagers either, say, "All that matters is that we love each other. The rest will work itself out." But that just is not true. Things don't just work themselves out; *you* have to work them out, and it can be hard work sometimes.

D: One great thing about courtship is that it allows you to have a love-filled relationship before marriage, yet at the same time maintain a focus on the important questions that need to be answered in preparation for marriage.

What kind of questions ought to be discussed?

J: We don't intend to give hints on arranging a wedding and things like that, but we do want to offer some advice about the practical things that guys and girls need to think about in preparing for marriage.

D: Keep in mind that all of these ideas are great topics to discuss when you are doing some of the character-building activities we discussed -- you might even ask these of your mentor, parents and other older couples with whom you visit.

Danielle, what are the issues girls ought to consider in preparing for marriage?

D: Young women can learn much from Titus 2:3-5, which tells older women to teach younger women how to love their husbands and children, be self-controlled and pure, be busy at home, be kind, and be subject to their husbands. I think this is an excellent framework, so let's go through them one by one.

1. *Loving your husband.*
   ▸ What are your future husband's goals for his life?
   ▸ List some ways you can support your husband in his goals.
   ▸ Interview some married women for ideas on how they demonstrate love for their husbands.

2. *Loving your children.*
   ▸ Do you know basic child care?
   ▸ What role will you play in your child's development?
   ▸ Will you home school, or send your child to a public or private school? Become familiar with different types of schooling. Attend a home school conference to see what materials are available for teaching your child, even if you don't intend to do that full time.
   ▸ How will you handle the discipline of your child? Consider reading a book or two about child training from a Christian perspective.
   ▸ Do a study of child training from the Bible, starting with Proverbs 22:6 ("Train up a child . . .").

3. *Being self-controlled and pure.*
   ▸ Do you have a daily schedule that you follow regularly? Consider reading a book on time management.
   ▸ Do you set goals as to what you want to accomplish each day? Have you ever set *long-term* goals? Try it out!
   ▸ Do you actively try to learn new things and put them into practice?
   ▸ What are you doing to develop godly character?
   ▸ In what areas do you struggle with emotional and physical purity?

4. *Being busy at home.*
   ▸ Do you know how to plan menus, cook, and serve food? If not, spend time learning from someone who is good at it.
   ▸ How do you want your home to be decorated? What styles do you prefer?
   ▸ Do you know how to budget and handle finances?

- ► What standards do you have for the cleanliness of your home?
- ► Do you know basic home maintenance?
- ► Do you know basic auto maintenance (i.e. how to change a tire)?

5. *Being kind.*
- ► Do you recognize your own daily and monthly cycles well enough to know when you are likely to be emotionally tired, and perhaps unkind?
- ► Do you purposefully practice kindness every day?
- ► What kind of words come out of your mouth? Are they demeaning or uplifting?

6. *Being subject to your husband.*
- ► Are you prepared to trust your husband's decisions, especially when they will dramatically affect your own life (i.e. where to go to church, how to handle finances, etc.)?
- ► What does "submission" mean?
- ► When might you, based on what you know about the guy already, be challenged to love him "as to the Lord"?
- ► Think about several ways you can "become one" with your husband (outside of your physical relationship).
- ► Talk with older women about how to develop oneness with your mate.

Wow! That's quite a list! Isn't that a little much?

D: I'm not saying that you must master each item on it. Nor am I saying that if you follow the list you will be ready for marriage! But it is a good place to start. Much of marriage is very *practical* and *ordinary*. If you know how to handle basic situations, it is easier to keep the "spark" alive which makes marriage fun and exciting.

But how does this list apply to young women who plan to work?

D: It applies whether you plan to work or not. Young married women often stay in the work force to gain life experience and get the "budget" on track. But it is still the case that the wife will have the greatest responsibility for maintaining the home, even if the husband helps out. Since Jeff and I have been married, I have been learning to serve in a variety of ways: helping out in Jeff's ministry, speaking, helping needy people through a social service agency, assisting my neighbor with child and home care, packing books for Summit Ministries to ship, and learning how to be a server in a local restaurant. We don't see any of these things as permanent, however. When we have children, my primary focus will be child rearing. It's the greatest possible ministry I can think of.

Okay, Jeff. What are the steps of preparation for guys?

J: Outside of emotional preparation, there are many practical questions to be addressed. Your father, her father and your mentor can help you understand what these steps involve. The point of this exercise is not to scare you away from marriage, or to say that you must have mastered all of these things before marriage. But it *is* intended to open your eyes to some of the responsibilities of marriage.

1. Relationship-building.
   ▸ Do you know what your bride-to-be really wants out of life?

- What are your (and her) expectations for marriage?
- How much time do your married friends spend working on relationship issues? Should they spend more? If so, doing what?
- What things could you do to make your wife happy?
- What things could you do to give your wife a feeling of security, both relationally and financially?

2. *Children.*
   - Are you prepared for having children? How many children? When? What will you do if have an "unplanned" pregnancy? (There is no such thing as guaranteed conception control).
   - Have you thought about or received counsel on the biblical and ethical issues surrounding birth control?
   - Have you visited with any fathers about the responsibilities of raising children?
   - What part will you take in raising your children, including teaching, disciplining and caring for them?
   - What additional expenses will you incur should your wife become pregnant? Are you prepared?

3. *Education.*
   - What do you want to do as a career?
   - Why have you chosen that career?
   - What kind of education do you need to do that?
   - Where will you get the necessary education?
   - How much will that education cost (in time and money)?
   - What will you have to sacrifice in order to pursue that career?

4. *Employment.*
   - What leads do you have for getting a job once your

education is complete?
- ► What qualities do you have that a potential employer might find valuable?
- ► What can you do to make yourself more qualified for employment (besides education)?
- ► What is your plan should you lose your job?

5. *Finances.*
- ► Do you have a plan for making enough money to support a wife and at least one child?
- ► Do you have a three-month reserve of money in the bank in case of an emergency?
- ► What are your long-term financial goals (i.e. house, college for your children, and retirement)? What are you doing right now to plan for them?
- ► Do you intend to buy a house? If so, do you have a workable plan for saving the money needed? Ask a Realtor to give you some materials and explain the procedures.
- ► Have you thought through a biblical perspective on debt? Have you carefully considered how much money you will spend on interest if you get a home or car loan?

6. *Home and auto maintenance.*
- ► What is your perspective on "stuff"? (i.e. boats, campers, motorcycles, etc.). Have you considered the cost for owning and maintaining these things?
- • Do you know how to change tires, oil, fluids, battery, spark plugs, etc.? What will you do if your car breaks down? How much will it cost to have a reliable car?
- • How will you protect your wife if your car breaks down while she is driving it?
- ► How much time and money does it take to care for a house? Ask a homeowner to help you detail this.

- ▸ Do you know how to fix things that break? (i.e. windows, doors, faucets, the furnace, furniture, etc.)
- ▸ Do you know basic remodeling techniques?

That list seems even more overwhelming. How does a person learn all of these things?

D: The list *is* extensive. That's one reason it is so vital to have a good relationship with your parents or mentor. My mentor helped me learn how to plan a menu on a budget (we knew our finances would be tight), and taught me helpful ideas for keeping an orderly home. I have also helped others with child care, house cleaning, washing and ironing, and menu planning and cooking. These were all great experiences. They allowed me to get a feel for what it's *like* to run a household with several children. I learned what kinds of things you face each day and even thought some about what I would do differently. If necessary, and if your parents approve, consider *living* with another family for a while. I did this for the month before our marriage, and really learned a lot.

J: The same is true for guys. Find opportunities to learn skills you need to fix things around the house, make improvements, and serve your wife. You cannot do this on your own no matter how skillful you are. God's system of learning from others works a lot better than the trial and error system we would otherwise use!

D: Now that we've listed the kinds of things you need to *think* through before marriage, it is time to list the kinds of things you need to *talk* through. That's what we'll do in the next chapter.

Chapter Thirteen

Getting Ready, Part Two: Stuff to Talk About

In addition to your individual preparation for becoming a husband or wife, is there something you should be doing together?

J: In our opinion, yes. There are many things you can discuss, most of them very practical, which will make the transition to marriage easier.

D: We've got to make a warning here, however. These questions are designed to help you get to know each other better. Don't use them to try and define every place the two of you are different. It is good to understand differences, but we must recognize that marriage involves *appreciating* the differences and loving each other *in spite* of them. It also involves learning to change. If you start drawing lines in the sand and saying, "This is the way I am, like it or not," you're in trouble.

J: These questions are in what we consider to be the five most significant categories of life outside of your relationship with God: Relationship, Family, Money, Time, and Space.

Relationship

▸ What are the things you do that your beloved finds most encouraging? Most bothersome?

▸ How should disputes in public be handled?

▸ Do you know your beloved's priorities? Could you list them?

▸ How would you like your beloved to respond when you are upset?

▸ What is "off-limits" in fighting?

▸ Which "good manners" are important to your beloved? Do you practice them?

▸ What is your beloved's favorite way to relax?

▸ How will you react when there is no gas in the car and you are already late for a meeting?

▸ How will you react when your beloved is late picking you up?

▸ What happens when you reach a stalemate in discussion?

▸ What is the best way for someone to compliment you in a meaningful way? What is the best compliment for your beloved?

▸ When do you most want your beloved with you? When do you most want to be alone?

▸ How important is it to have a specific "date night" when you are married?

▸ In what areas would you like your beloved to keep you accountable? How would you like to be kept accountable in those areas?

- What should your beloved know that you are sensitive about?
- What expectations do you have about marriage?
- What are three things you consider most important when making decisions?

Family

- What family traditions would you like to keep?
- How important is it to see your family *on* a holiday? How important is it to celebrate the holidays with your family?
- What holidays are most important to spend together?
- Is it more important to you or to your family that you spend holidays together?
- What is the limit on how often family members may come stay with you after you are married?
- When a problem arises with one of your families, who should be your "spokesperson"?
- When your parents are no longer able to care for themselves, what responsibilities should you and your spouse take in caring for them?
- In what areas should families be allowed to step into the decision-making process? To what extent?
- What should be taken into consideration when making decisions about families?
- What do you plan to do differently from the way your family did things?

Money

- Each of you record your spending for a month. Look at each other's lists and discuss.
- Prepare a budget proposal for after you are married. Make sure everything is included. Discuss it.

- What do you do with "extra" money (e.g. left-over grocery money)?
- When you don't have enough money for something, do you take money from another fund, withdraw from savings, buy it on credit, or go without?
- How often should the checkbook be balanced? Who will do it?
- What are the three things you consider most important in finances?
- What are some things you currently buy (include everything: magazine subscriptions, CDs, certain brands of clothing, etc.) that you would be unwilling to quit buying once married. Go shopping with each other, buying the things you would ordinarily buy (especially things like health/beauty products).
- Go furniture shopping together, pretending that you each have $10,000 to spend. Make your choices separately and compare notes. Discuss why you made those choices, and think about what styles you each prefer.
- What situations would merit the wife getting a part-time or full-time job?
- Is getting a loan ever justified? Under what circumstances, if any?
- Is a tithe mandatory? How much? To the church only or also to other causes?

Time

- What do you consider a waste of time?
- Do you ever just waste time? What is your favorite way to waste time?
- How much time do you allow for reading each week? When?
- What kinds of books do you most like to read? What kinds

do you refuse to read and why? Do you believe that no one should read certain books?

- How much time would you like to spend discussing the relationship? What do you consider "working" on the relationship? (i.e. would reading "relationship" books count?)
- If a friend asks you to do something spontaneous but you have time planned with your beloved, what do you do?
- Do you ask your beloved's permission to see certain people or just go? Do you ask permission to go certain places (i.e. a movie, shopping, or mountain biking)? Would that change after marriage?
- Write out what you consider to be realistic weekly schedules and compare.
- What is important in the time you spend exclusively together?
- What is important in the time spent with others?
- What interests would you like to share?
- What interests do you prefer to pursue alone?

Space

- What is necessary for a place to seem like home to you?
- What things are most important in having a clean house?
- What would you be willing to give up, space-wise and cleanliness-wise?
- Who should take care of what housekeeping responsibilities?
- Draw floor plans of your ideal homes and compare.
- Describe your tastes in architecture.
- Describe your "dream estate."
- How important is it that you have time alone each day?
- What are some important considerations in organizing your space?

- ▸ What rituals do you go through before starting on a business trip? Going to bed? Going on vacation? Getting ready in the morning? Do you prefer to talk or not talk at those times?
- ▸ What would you most like to share with your beloved?

That ought to about cover it!

D: Actually, it doesn't. But it is a great place to start. You'll know a whole lot more about the person after going through just a few of these questions.

J: Now that we've gone through all of our practical ideas, we want to share with you the feedback that we've received, from all kinds of audiences, and attempt to answer some of the difficult questions that have come up.

Chapter Fourteen
Ladies and Gentlemen, The Question Is . . .

Since our own courtship, and since we have been speaking
on the subject together, hundreds of young people have come to
believe that courtship is God's best for their lives, and have
committed to putting these principles into practice. However,
difficult questions often arise. Here are some of the questions
we've had so far, as well as some of our ideas on how they
might be answered.

What if my parents are forcing me to "do courtship"?

This is a tough one! If you're doing courtship because your
parents want you to, you may sometimes feel like referring
to it as "this crazy idea that my nutty parents dreamed up
since they couldn't legally keep me locked in the attic."
Your frustration is understandable, at least as far as you feel
like you're "missing out" on something good by not dating.
One teenage girl told us, "You're lucky because at least you

had dating experiences in your life before deciding on courtship." Here's our advice:

1. Don't regret not trying dating. You may know in your heart that courtship is better than dating, that dating will produce heartache, that it is settling for less than the best, and that it will draw your emotions away from spending your time the way you should. But you still want to try it. If so, here's an important lesson: you don't have to *try* something to know it is not good, just as you don't have to hit yourself in the foot with a sledge hammer to know it will hurt. Take it from those who have tried it! The true winners in life are the ones who don't feel compelled to recreate the mistakes of others. They *learn* from the lessons of others and have a better life for it.

2. Listen to your parents. You did not get your parents by accident! God chooses our parents, not us. It may be hard to believe this, but the fact that your parents have set standards for you shows that they really do have your best interests at heart. This does not mean that parents never make mistakes. It means that God blesses us when we obey, and the Bible clearly says that you should obey and honor your parents (Ephesians 6:1-3), that "it may go well with you." Trust God to do the right thing through your parents. You can't lose; you will be blessed by God whether they are right or wrong!

3. Be positive. There are some things in life we can't change. Successful people recognize those things and use them to their advantage. For example, we can't change the law of gravity. There are two ways to respond to this. You could get really ticked off and try to break it, or you could recognize that it exists whether you like it or not and then *incorporate* it into your way of thinking. People in the first group are more likely to jump out of tall buildings! People in the second group use the law of gravity to their advantage, and live healthier, happier lives. Instead of moping around the house, use your time to invest in the lives of others. Work to make an impact on the world around you. God brought the two of us together when we were both in the middle of doing what He wanted us to do. His timing was perfect, and we didn't have to regret the way we spent our time before we got married.

I don't see what's so bad about just going out on innocent dates with pretty girls (or handsome guys).

This is always a hard question to answer. In a purely practical sense, there is nothing wrong with it, assuming no immorality occurs. But we have to ask the question, "Why?" Is it because of peer pressure to have a girlfriend or boyfriend? Is it because you want to be seen with someone who is attractive? Is it because you want someone who is attractive to pay attention to you?

To us, the key phrase is, "What's so bad about . . ." People usually ask that question when they are contemplating doing something they know they shouldn't, like, "What's so bad about French kissing?" and so on. Many people spend their whole lives trying to see how close they can get to being "bad" while still being "good."

Isn't it funny that successful athletes never ask questions like that? You never hear them ask the coach, "How many practices can I skip and still be on the team?" or "How few minutes can I spend in the weight room and still be in shape?" Successful athletes aren't focused on how little they can do, they want to win the prize! They *want* to do everything they possibly can to succeed. As Christians, we are told to "run in such a way as to get the prize" (I Corinthians 9:24). Our lives are to be proactive, looking ahead rather than behind. A proactive person can *choose* to invest the time, energy and money he would otherwise spend on a date to accomplish something more worthwhile or to develop relationships with lots of people, including family.

Are you saying I can't spend time with people of the opposite sex?

No! In fact, we have given several ideas in this book about to spend time with other people. Here is a good rule of thumb: before you have committed to marriage, all Christian guys and girls are brothers and sisters in Christ. So *do* the kind of things you *would* do with your brother or sister and *don't* do the kind of things you *wouldn't* do with your brother or sister.

Even though I mostly do things in groups, I still experience temptation. How do I deal with this?

Usually temptation comes when you begin to "pair off," even when you are still formally in groups. We suggest first of all that you share the fact that you are experiencing temptation with your parents or mentor. Ask them to pray for you and give you suggestions about avoiding temptation.

In addition to accountability, here are two ideas for handling temptation. First, avoid tempting situations.

Dr. Lee Griffith, psychology professor at Anderson University suggests these tips:

1. *Go places in the day time.*
2. *Stay in groups.*
3. *Plan your time in advance.*
4. *Keep good-byes short.*
5. *Avoid private places.*
6. *Avoid being in either of your homes without other people being there.*
7. *Make sure your parents approve of the time you're spending together, and know what you're up to.*

Second, go on the offense. Do this by "taking every thought captive" to the obedience of Christ (II Corinthians 10:5). Maintaining a pure mind is one of the hardest things to do in life, even for grown men and women. Memorizing Scripture verses that you can meditate on when you are tempted will turn your attention *away* from temptation and *toward* Christ. For example, Job made a covenant with his eyes that he would not look lustfully at women (Job 31:1). Write that covenant on a card, making it your own commitment.

What do I say if someone asks me out?

Here are some ideas that will give you a sense of how to respond when someone asks you out. You can modify them to meet your needs.

- "I'm really honored that you would ask me, but since I'm only young once I've decided to try and spend my time with a lot of people, rather than go out on dates

- one-on-one. Would you like to come along with my other friends and _____?"

- "Thank you for asking, but you know, I'm really close to my family, and I would prefer that you spend some time with my father and my family as a way of getting to know you better."

- "I appreciate your asking. It sounds like fun. But I'm not ready to spend time with just one person. Can we get a whole group together to do it?"

- "Wow, that really sounds good. But I've already got plans that evening to spend time with my family. Would you like to come along? We're going to _____."

- "Thank you for asking, but I've decided not to date one-on-one until I'm more ready to get married. I'd still like to spend time with you, though. Would you be interested in joining our youth group? We like to do things together as a group."

- "You know, what I really like to do before spending time with someone is have them get to know my father. Why don't you come over? He's a really great guy."

- "I'm sorry, I'm not able to do that. But I do have plans to take a group of my friends downtown to _____. Would you like to come?"

I'm not ready to begin courting or planning for marriage. What should I do in the meantime?

That's a great question! Since dating is such an integral part of our culture, we sometimes have a hard time figuring out what to do *besides* dating. First, relax. You have opportunities to accomplish things *now* that you will never have again. Take advantage of them: join a speech or debate team, work on a political campaign, get involved helping those less fortunate than you, or start a business. Does this mean you should never have fun? No! When you're ready to relax (relaxing is more meaningful when you've worked hard), try some of the character-building ideas we've listed or make up some of your own. The key point is this: make your time count. Focus on building relationships with lots of people, both family and friends. God will reward this with a stronger sense of purpose in life, and the time before you get married will pass much more quickly!

My parents are divorced. How does this affect my courtship opportunities?

If your family has been hurt by the pain of divorce, you are well aware of the devastation it can cause. It can also make your own relationships more difficult because it damages the natural accountability system God put in place. So, courtship is more difficult when you're family is not together, but it is not impossible. If your father or mother cannot be relied on for accountability, then seek a mentoring relationship with your pastor, his wife, or other role models in your church. The Bible says that widows and the fatherless should be taken care of by the church. Your pastor actually becomes like a surrogate father to you, helping you make wise decisions.

By the way, if your parents are still together, thank them for their commitment to each other. Their example and the habits you learned from them will help strengthen your own marriage!

My father or mother is not a Christian. How does this affect courtship?

If your father or mother are not Christians, they may not understand your desire to maintain purity and accountability in relationships. But it is our guess that they are still interested in your success, and will help you where they can. Even if they do not have a personal relationship with Jesus Christ, God still gives them the wisdom to see many of the obstacles and challenges you will face.

Moreover, never does Scripture tell us to *stop* honoring our parents just because they are not believers. The integrity you demonstrate in your courtship relationship, and in being kind to your parents and honoring them, will be the strongest testimony you have ever delivered. At the same time, if your parents are not providing the spiritual accountability you need, make an appointment to discuss this with your pastor. He is responsible for helping you develop spiritually, and can help you find answers.

I'm already in a relationship. What do I do?

One of our greatest fears as human beings is losing those whom we have come to depend on. Being in a relationship gives comfort and security, and it makes you feel good about yourself. Perhaps you're afraid that if you try to turn your relationship into a courtship, you'll lose the other person.

First, talk to your parents and listen to their advice. Most likely, they will be willing to back you up in your conviction about courtship. Second, share your conviction about courtship with the other person, describing what it means and how it would change your relationship, and then asking for feedback. Explain that you want your relationship to be accountable to parents, especially your fathers, and that you want the relationship to focus on building character.

It is our experience that once you explain all this, you will know right away if this is also the conviction of the other person. If the other person quickly loses interest in you, or balks at your suggestions, it is likely that 1) they need more time to think it through, or 2) they are *not* the person God has for you. Whatever you do, don't let them talk you out of your commitment by saying things like, "C'mon. Don't be so serious. It's not that big of a deal." Stick to your guns.

I now recognize that my current relationship is not honoring to God. What do I do?

As we mentioned in the previous question, losing a relationship is one of the hardest things to do. If you have been convicted that your current relationship is not honoring to God, then it usually means that serious changes must take place in the relationship, or you must end it, as hard as that may be. What should you do?

First, consult with your parents. Parents can almost always detect whether your relationships with others are healthy or not. They can give you suggestions for how to approach the other person, or at least support you. Second, make a list of qualities that you would like to have in a marriage partner. Does this person match up? Are you really in the relationship because you believe this is the person God would have you marry? If not, are you in it because it is comfortable? Because it would be too hard to change?

If you believe that this is *not* the person God would have you marry, don't let any excuse get in your way. End the relationship. End it as gently as you can, but end it. Too many people get married to a person with all the wrong qualities and for all the wrong reasons. These marriages seldom last, and they produce heartache from beginning to end.

If you are a girl, your father should help you. If the guy persists in wanting to maintain the relationship, it is our belief that your father is responsible for helping you handle it. Your father should gently but firmly explain that his daughter has recognized that the relationship is not honoring to God, and that it must end. If your father wishes, he can offer to mentor the guy. But there should *never* be a promise, implicit or explicit, that this will restore the relationship with you.

I have already been involved physically with the person I am interested in. What do I do?

Refer to the answer above about avoiding temptation. If you have already been involved physically, it is *extremely* difficult to avoid temptation. *You will not be able to do it without accountability to your parents and pastor.* Don't mess around with this one. You *will* get burned if you do.

This may sound difficult, but we believe the only way to work through this issue is to start from scratch. Confess what you have done to God. I John 1:9 says that if we confess our sins, God is faithful and just and will forgive them and purify us. Next, you must restore honor and trust in the relationship by asking forgiveness from the other person. Ask them to participate in an accountability program with parents and mentors. Study the idea of courtship together at a time and place that will not invite temptation. If the other person does not come to the same convictions, it is best to break off the relationship completely.

If your relationship has led to a pregnancy, your responsibility is much greater. Consult with your parents and pastor for their advice as difficult as that may be. You cannot work through this on your own.

We want to say here that we worship a big God. He will forgive you for whatever you have done. If you make further mistakes, he will forgive those too. But God still allows us to experience the consequences of our sin. These consequences can lead even to pregnancy outside of marriage or incurable diseases. At very least, you will have emotional scars that will make it much more difficult for you to trust your future mate and to love him or her with your whole heart.

Chapter Fifteen
Happily Ever After

The fair maiden woke from her nightmare with a start. "That was just awful," she thought. *Her* knight in shining armor would never address her as 'babe' and suggest such unromantic things as the knight in her dream, would he?

As she flung open the windows, her heart stopped. There *was* a lone rider, far across the plain, galloping toward her father's castle. "How can I be sure that my nightmare was just a bad dream?" she wondered, her anticipation mixed with anxiety.

As the horseman spurred his fine white Arab charger closer, the sun glinted off his shining armor. It *was* him, of that the fair maiden was certain. But doubts continued to plague her mind. What if he forgot his promise to her father? What if he changed his mind? What if he lost the high ideals that had swept her off her feet?

The white charger's nostrils flared as his master urged him on in eager advance. It seemed like an eternity, but at last the knight reigned in his mount beneath her window. As he slowly raised his face shield, his fine features were illumined by the setting sun. The fair maiden held her breath.

"My love," exclaimed the knight gently, his eyes burning bright. "I have come, at last, just as I said I would."

Now *That's* More Like It

Choosing the person you will marry is the second most important decision of your life, next to having a personal relationship with Jesus Christ. For many, this is a bumpy road. Yes, there are stretches of great excitement, but they are punctuated by the pot holes of indecision, fear, and distrust.

Courtship does not guarantee a perfect relationship. It cannot promise freedom from trouble. But it *does* lay a strong foundation which will make things better than you ever imagined.

Courtship allows you to develop a relationship leading to marriage while maintaining and even improving your relationship with your parents and family. It offers protection and the opportunity to *really get to know the other person.* The self-control you develop will create trust in the relationship, leading to a marriage with no regrets. It passes a godly heritage of purity to your children.

You say it's old fashioned? It may be just that. But your decision to commit to courtship could also be one of the best decisions you will ever make. So, knights and fair maidens, you're off . . . on the journey of a lifetime!

Appendix
The Article that Started it All

Joshua Harris has graciously given us permission to reproduce this article, taken from the *New Attitude Magazine* (Volume 1, Number 2, 1993), a quarterly magazine designed especially for home school teenagers (write to them at P.O. Box 2250, Gresham, OR 97080 for more information).

This article gave the two of us a starting point for discussing courtship, and we ended up basing our relationship on it. We're glad to reproduce this article here in the hope that the discussion may continue and last at least as long as the pages in this book.

Dating Problems, Courtship Solutions
by Joshua Harris

A friend was telling me about the class of junior high girls she worked with at her church. "The most important things in the average junior high girl's life are clothes and having a boyfriend," she said. "Just the other day one of the girls called me. She was practically in tears saying, 'I don't have a boyfriend! I need a boyfriend!' I tried to calm her down and convince her it wasn't important but she wouldn't listen."

"How old is she?" I asked.

"Fourteen."

When it comes to relationships in America, teenagers are in a frenzy. Like crazed sharks, teens are in a state of confusion, grasping at anything and everything that promises fulfillment or happiness. This can be seen clearly in the institution called dating. "Dating is 'me' centered," says Debbie Lechner, an 18-year-old home schooler from Pennsylvania. In the dating system everybody has somebody - a boyfriend, a girlfriend. And if you don't, something is wrong with you.

"There is pressure in high school for you to have a boyfriend or girlfriend. It's just there," says Matt Dotson, a graduate of a public school. "Anyone who is looked at as 'cool' is going to have a boyfriend or girlfriend."

The dilemma serious Christian teens face is that most of the world, including a majority of the Christian community, has already determined that dating is a "nutritious part of this complete teenage experience." Home schooler Rebekah Garfield says, "Most of my friends date. It used to be real difficult because they were always wanting to fix me up with somebody or pushing me to go out with somebody."

But the Christian who sees the dating road littered with broken hearts and dotted with the pot holes and pitfalls of temptation must ask, "Is the dating road a detour from God's travel plans for my life?" and "Is there a better, safer road to marriage?"

A New Route

Recently Christian parents, along with their teens, have realized the need to remap the route to fruitful, God-ordained marriages. The result has been a push, particularly among home schoolers, to return to the more biblical principles of courtship.

Simply defined, courtship is a reformed version of dating under the supervision of parents between a man and a woman who are ready to marry in the near future. In consumer terms, contemporary dating is the equivalent to window shopping, and courtship is shopping cash in hand under the direction of experienced buyers. The term used is not important. What's important is that courtship bypasses the pitfalls of contemporary dating and provides a much safer, smoother ride to the union of man and wife.

Dating Problems; Courtship Solutions

The first major problem of dating is that it has very little to do with marriage. "The purpose of dating is to have a good time," says Bethany Albers, a senior at a small Christian school in Oregon. This means that for most people the dating road doesn't have a destination. Bethany explains, "The problem with not having a direction is that you're just kind of floating around. You don't have any definite guidelines, for instance, of where you're going to stop physically or how committed you're going to be even just emotionally."

Dating has always been a way for young people to experience the exciting, romantic side of a relationship without commitment or responsibility. A boyfriend/girlfriend relationship provides the feelings of intimacy and creates emotional "highs", ("Oh, when he says 'I love you' tingles run up my spine!") but it has nothing to hold it together. Because most teens who date are not in a position to marry, the relationship has nowhere to go. The result is that the relationship "peaks out" as dealing with physical temptation brought on by emotional intimacy becomes the focus of the relationship. Most couples break up at this point and move on to new relationships seeking the excitement of "falling in love." This kind of dating pattern is nothing more than a training ground for divorce. The person who falls into this cycle has given most of his heart away to others by the time he meets his spouse.

Courtship remedies this problem because it has a definite planning destination: life-long marriage. A person is ready to begin the process of courtship when he or she is ready to marry in the very near future. While you might date someone you have no long term interest in, you only court a person who has shown promise of possessing character qualities you and your parents have established as being important.

The decision of when a young person is ready for marriage is one that should be reached with the help of parents and based on certain criteria. Mike Farris, in his book *The Homeschooling Father,* says young men should be prepared for marriage in the three practical areas of: career and finances, home maintenance, and fatherhood. For girls the areas of practical preparation are: teaching, home-making and motherhood. Young men and women should not enter into courtship until they are prepared in each of these areas. These criteria obviously exclude a great number of teens.

Another advantage of courtship's clearly stated intent is that it avoids the "broken heart syndrome" associated with dating. Bethany Albers says this is worth avoiding. "When the one guy I dated seriously broke up with me, it was definitely the toughest thing that's ever happened to me."

Matt Dotson explains the outcome of the "going-out/breaking-up" cycle, "When you give someone your heart, it's different the next time around. You're leery, and in the back of your mind you're thinking, 'I don't want to do this because I don't want to get hurt again.'"

Because the goal in a courtship relationship is not to achieve emotional and physical intimacy, the couple can terminate a relationship without leaving a piece of their heart behind. The courtship relationship is not long term. You don't have a "steady courtship" for all of high school and two years of college. Courtship need only be as long as it takes to get to know a person and determine if he or she has certain characteristics. If the person lacks the qualities you're looking for, there is no reason to continue courtship.

The second major pitfall of dating is that it takes place outside of the home. The whole concept of a date or a dating relationship is two people being alone, isolated from the rest of the world. Whether the two find their isolation in the anonymity of a public place or on the telephone, their goal is privacy. The result is that the couple becomes isolated from family, friends, and even God as their lives begin to revolve around the relationship. Rebekah Garfield observes, "There is almost always a breakdown in your relationship with God even if that's not your intention. Your focus becomes pleasing that person and doing stuff with them."

This isolation often leads to sexual temptation. "You're alone too much," says Dotson. "You're automatically going to go down hill. It opens the door physically." God's Word tells us clearly in II Timothy 2:22 to "Flee the evil desires of youth", not get as close as possible. Dating separates two people from the protection of those who love them the most and sets them up to fail.

Because courtship brings the process back into the home, it protects the couple from much of the temptation of physical involvement.

For the person ready for marriage and looking for a partner, dating's third major problem can be dangerous; dating creates an artificial environment for two people to get to know each other. Rebekah laughs when she thinks of the dating relationships around her. "My friends' dating relationships are real superficial a lot of times. They're just putting on a show to impress the other person."

In a dating relationship the guy and girl are not only on their best behavior, but they are also removed from those who really know them, their families. In a dating relationship it's easy to make a good impression, that is in fact, a false impression.

Courtship takes place under the guidance of both families and in the setting of home life. This keeps the couple from being wrapped up in themselves and helps them to see their relationship in the context of real life.

The mistaken idea many have is that the teenager who rejects the dating system has to avoid friendship with members of the opposite sex. This is not the case. "My family goes by the courtship idea and just recently I've really committed myself to that," says Rebekah Garfield. But Rebekah still has friendships with guys. "I have lots and lots of guy friends," she says. "I have some really great relationships with guys just on the friendship level."

In these friendships it is vital that the teenager and his or her parents are working as a team. Honest communication and submission to parental authority and judgment keep relationships protected. "If a guy comes along and wants to date me, I direct him to my father," says Rebekah. "If you don't have a relationship with your parents, forget about keeping a courtship commitment."

Once parents and teens start working together they can develop ways to have protected relationships. "I feel very strongly that the whole involvement of family relationships and hospitality has to take place," says Linda Werner, a home schooling mother of two teens. "Parents have to reach out to other families that have kids and make an effort to get out and do things as groups in a family context."

Utilizing Youth

Finally, courtship allows the teenager to wisely utilize the energy and relative freedom the teenage years provide. Instead of wasting energy on short-term dating relationships, many teenagers are realizing courtship allows them to focus on preparation for life, and being ready for marriage. "For me courtship means I can be free until I'm ready to get married," says Rebekah. "I don't have to concentrate on looking for the right person, because I know God is going to bring the right person along."

"I don't consider courtship old-fashioned," says Rebekah. "I have many friends that are doing it, and I've seen the success that a lot of them who are now married have had. Most people that are critical of courtship just want to date, and they're not looking for alternatives. They're going to have a critical perspective. Their focus isn't in the right place. They want to satisfy themselves."

Ultimately, courtship is a change of attitude toward relationships. The courtship attitude not only alters the way you look for a spouse; it changes the way you treat members of the opposite sex. Serious Christian teens must realize that the boyfriend/girlfriend exclusiveness of the dating system is based on a self-seeking, pleasure-seeking attitude toward relationships. It is an attitude that is unwilling to wait for the emotional and physical gratification of marriage. On the other hand, the attitude of courtship is one of patience and waiting for the Lord's perfect plan. It is not some evil concoction invented by parents to keep something good from their children. Instead, courtship is a smarter, more biblical way to choose a life partner and relate to members of the opposite sex. Not centered on self, it seeks to bless others, not use them. The dating road is not the only road. God has given young people a better route that not only leads to the right destination, but also helps make the teenage years the best they can be.

Of Knights and Fair Maidens
makes a great gift for youth, pastors and parents

3 ways to order:

1. Visit www.myersinstitute.com and order using your credit card or check.

2. Complete and mail order form below with your check or money order.

3. Call toll-free (888) 792-4445, to use Visa or MasterCard.

Of Knights and Fair Maidens makes a great gift for youth, pastors and parents

3 ways to order:

1. Visit www.myersinstitute.com and order using your credit card or check.

2. Complete and mail order form below with your check or money order.

3. Call toll-free (888) 792-4445, to use Visa or MasterCard.

Of Knights and Fair Maidens   ($8.95 each) $ _____

Courtship: Our Story (45 Min. tape of Jeff & Danielle)   ($5.95 each) $ _____

Shipping: (per item, either book or tape) $ _____

1	=	$3.00
2 to 5 items	=	$1.50 each
6 to 10 items	=	$1.00 each
11 to 20 items	=	.85 each
21 & up items	=	.70 each

Total: $ _____

2002 prices and content subject to change without notice.

Name _____

Address _____

City, State and Zip Code _____

Telephone _____

Send to:
Myers Institute
P.O. Box 7 • Dayton, TN 37321

NOTES: